My Friend, The Sun

"Nature is yours and mine..."

Mary Emeji

To Jammes Henry
keep skinning!
ll~~ 30/7/14

GlintingBlue Press

ISBN: 978-0-9928162-2-3
MMXVI

Printed and bound in Great Britain.
First published in Great Britain in 2016
By
GlintingBlue Press
glintingbluepress1@yahoo.co.uk

CONTENTS

JOYS OF THE SUN

RELATIONSHIP WITH THE SUN

THE SUN RENEWS

SEASONS OF LIFE

THE SUN AND FAMILY

THE SUN TRANSCENDS

ABOUT THE AUTHOR

Mary Emeji is the Poet Laureate of Luton appointed by the Mayor in 2012 and Founder of Luton Poetry Society since 2011, who coordinates monthly poetry events at Luton Central Library. A double law graduate with LLB (Hons) and LLM Commercial Law (with Distinction) from University of Bedfordshire, Mary's passion for poetry has led her to frequently write and perform in libraries, poetry groups, festivals and events around the U.K and abroad. The 'six books in six years' poet laureate is a regular guest on BBC Three Counties Radio, who's been regularly featured in local papers and magazines including Luton-At-Large, University of Bedfordshire LIFE, Luton on Sunday, Luton News and Herald & Post. On being short-listed for poetry competitions, Mary's poems were published in the National Poetry Anthology *'A Gathering Of Minds' (United Press 2012)* and *'I Believe' (United Press 2013 – a religious anthology)*. She was selected as one of the 'Top Ten Poets in the UK' and published in anthology *'Ten Of The Best' (United Press 2013)*. Mary's luminous poem *'The Angel Star'* won the National Poetry Day competition run by Bedfordshire Libraries in 2012. Her poetry collections are available at many bookshops and online retailers including Amazon, Waterstones, and libraries. Copies autographed by Mary are available directly from her websites (at discounted rate): www.lutonpoetrysociety.com and www.maryemeji.ning.com

OTHER BOOKS BY MARY

THE BOND OF LOVE (2009 – Shieldcrest Publishers) – Mary's debut collection of poems about love, friendship, family, drawing on the happiness, challenges and triumphs of true love.
THE LOVE OF GOD (2010 – Shieldcrest Publishers) – Collection of inspirational Christian poems and nature poems, useful for healing and rejuvenation.
ROYAL LUMINOSITY (2011 – United Press) - Dedicated to Prince William and Princess Catherine, this book received a royal acknowledgement from Her Majesty, The Queen in 2011.
TIMELESS DATE (2012 – GlintingBlue Press) - Co-written with her favourite Bard William Shakespeare, these poems create a time-travel through words to discover a deep connection between Will and Mary!
FUNDAMENTALITY (2013 – GlintingBlue Press) – Poems on self-reflection, meditation, inner peace, and motivation to stay strong through the seasons of life.
PULCHRITUDE (2014 – GlintingBlue Press) – From the Latin 'Pulcher' meaning 'Beauty', this book reveals the beauty of life, love, nature and the world around us!

PREFACE

Three years ago on 20th July 2013, Mary had a unique encounter with the Sun whilst doing the dishes and looking out of the kitchen window. The rest is history. This book reveals a unique friendship between Mary and the Sun whom she describes as the source of light, warmth and energy not just for us humans but for all God's creation. Mary loves to sit in the sun, with the sun, and think....and talk.

This extraordinary realm of elevation, connection and creativity is indeed what poetry is all about. Mary's love for the sun stems from her love for God, the giver of true light. She describes Jesus as her "inward sun" who constantly shines, despite the fluctuating seasons of life.

The poems in this book are filled with light and perception of the wonderful nature all around us and they implore the reader to find light, warmth and energy even in darkest vale. A candle lit is fuelled and sustained from inside, and not from fluctuating winds that blow all around. Noticeably, the sun appears on the pages of this book, to imprint on its reader's mind.

Scientifically, the Sun accounts for 99.86% of the mass in the solar system. The Sun provides a vital ingredient for most of the life on earth. Without the energy provided through sunlight, vegetation cannot grow and without vegetation, man and other animals will have no source of nourishment. The sun is over 4,660 million years old, with a temperature of 10 million degrees at its core and 5,800 degrees on surface, and the earth is second to the nearest planet to the sun.

The relationship between Mary and the Sun radiates through the lines of the poems in a bright, warm, and enchanting way. Such enchantment that lingers long after the book closes, and the dreams begin!

After the rain, comes sunshine.
Nothing is hidden under the sun.
There's light at a tunnel's end to find,
And after each night, comes a new dawn!

FOREWORD

In Mary Emeji's book 'My Friend, The Sun', Mary engages with the sun to explore her faith. As the sun is the nearest star, approximately 93 million miles from the earth, it gives light and warmth to the earth, nourishes the humans and all living beings, and through photosynthesis enables life. In her opening verses, she talks of God giving the 'new day' and 'the days unfold in turns' and 'the birds of night have gone in flight'. This builds us into the relationship with the sun and moon. They are the measure of life, like 'music across the universe'. There is an essential call:
'Be wise with time each minute, each second.
Be all that you dream, to none - a second!'

The varying colours of the rainbow become the 'Gifts of the Spirit', for example, violet, 'the fear of God, brings lasting gleam surmounting rays where Wisdom begins'. A new relationship is formed with Nature, which may be reflected in our daily rituals, for example, the joy of horse riding:
'The Sun shines on, illuminating her skin,
from pores to veins to thoughts within,
to the soul where God's light elevates'.

Mary varies her diffused styles with an acrostic poem 'BEYOND' and three Sonnets including 'Ensconced' her dialogue with William Shakespeare drawing from his Sonnets, on a coffee date. She previously wrote a book in conjunction with Shakespeare entitled 'Timeless Date'. The Sun's energy fires us to new heights and like King Solomon, the new movie 'Lucy' predicts the possibility of brain capacity arriving at 100%. Finally, the whole canopy of the Sun, Moon and Stars reflects the glory of Mary, the Mother of God, who bore her Son to redeem the World.

Mary who began writing poems at a young age has in this book shown her capabilities and coherence by employing a thematic approach to her study of the Sun, our relationship with it and its effect on the earth and its seasons which lead us to the conclusion that the 'Sun transcends'. There is a theological dimension right here. May the Sun shine on this little book offering!

Alan Rainer, Poet, Philosopher,
(June 2016)

REVIEWS

Mary Emeji is a prolific poet and the life and soul of Luton Poetry Society, and her enthusiasm for poetry shows why it was a good decision to make her Luton Poet Laureate. She charms and enchants us with her appearance, personality and theatrical performances of poems, sometimes accompanied by lovely well-chosen music. Her excellent recall enables her to perform from memory and act it out, thereby enhancing the experience for others. She even entertains and delights us with annual "Be A Poet – History Comes Alive" meetings where she has played a Doctor Who-like role travelling through time with a special torch and exciting background music to bring back great poets of the past (really us members in costume) to perform once again in the present. A starring role in Doctor Who, perhaps even as the next Doctor, surely beckons!
Francis McDonnell, Poet, Mathematician,
Author of "The Alien That Came To Dinner."

Mary's poetry has an enchanting flow and an arresting rhythm. When a reader gets into the zone of this writing, he or she will feel these qualities as strongly as when Mary performs her work, which she does wonderfully.
Neil Rowland, Poet, Novelist and Writer

Mary's new collection reaffirms her poetic sensitivity to issues and events that many can relate to. Her spirituality is harnessed in the writing of poems about our inner lives; and her observational skills of the visible world provide complimentary texts that are equally pleasurable to read.
James Henry, Poet and Wordsmith

I am very impressed with the amount of work Mary has done in a relatively short time to promote the work of poetry in Luton. We do need to raise the profile of our poets in Luton, and she has done a lot to make that happen.
Cllr. Syd Knight (Mayor of Luton 2012 –2013)

NOTE FROM THE COUNTESS OF ERROLL

"Mary is an inspirational poet, her poetry conveys good traditional values and her words flow from the heart. I feel privileged to have met the Poet Laureate of Luton. Mary's faith and commitment to poetry will give pleasure to many readers in the future."

Lady Isabelle Erroll,
30th June 2016

ACKNOWLEDGEMENTS

All praise and glory to God the Light of my life and maker of the **Sun**. To my beloved family and friends, anything is possible under the **Sun**. To my friend, the **Sun**…you in me and me in you is you in you and me in me.

Taking from the opening lines of the Italian classical duet which Mary loves, **'Pur Ti Miro'** by **Claudio Monteverdi**:

Mary: Pur ti miro, pur ti godo
I gaze on you, I delight in you

Sun: Pur ti stringo, pur t'annondo
I embrace you, I enchant you

DEDICATION

To Mary Mother of God, the woman clothed with the Sun, standing on the Moon and wearing a crown of twelve Stars!

(Book of Revelation Chapter 12:1)

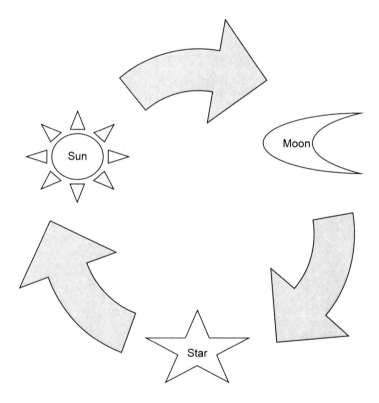

THE SUN CHART

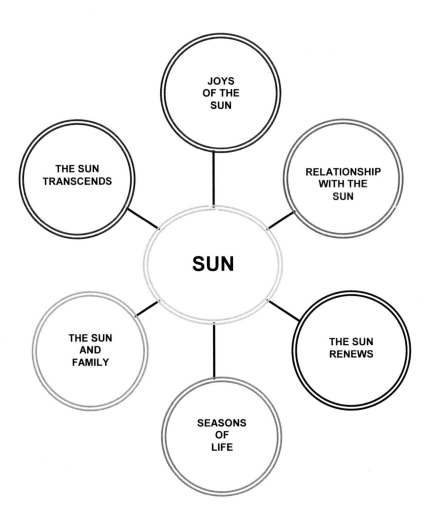

JOYS OF THE SUN

FOUR ZEROS

At this moment of four zeros,
What am I feeling inside?
A new day that God bestows?
A chance to swim in the tide?

For each road leads into the next
And the days unfold in turns:
Sometimes in clear, colourful text,
Other times in puzzle that spurns.

(7th October 2013, at midnight 00:00)

RISING

Parches of clouds spread over
The light blue sky
On a summer afternoon.
I see you
In the brightening trees,
My sun coming through.

ALL ALIGHT

See the light.
Feel delight.
At peace with sight,
Increased in might.

Come alight
On gardens bright,
For dim is fright
When all feels right.

The birds of night
Have gone in flight,
And you're on height
To new sunlight.

LAYERS

Layers of white clouds spread across the blue sky,
Layers of roses attracting travellers by.
Layers of me wrapped around your finger,
Layers of sunrays infusing the thinker.

Layers of words streaming from heaven,
Layers of rain moistening the garden.
Layers of thoughts to places near and far,
Layers of past love drifted apart.

Layers of poems, layers of words,
Layers of places to worship my God.
Layers of me in layers of me,
Layers of finding where I should be.

Layers of tasks, layers of plans,
Layers of butter on gingerbread man.
Layers of struggle, layers of faith,
Layers of glory reaching heaven's gate.

ANGEL FORECAST

I was told for fact, that an Angel will visit
Sometime, somewhere – I didn't know for how long,
But I knew deep inside I couldn't resist
To keep her with me where she'd belong.

For heaven on earth is heaven profound,
Not searched for, but seen through Angel's eyes.
The Light and Joy and Peaceful sound
All came in my bundle of sweet surprise.

My Angel shines like the timeless sun
And a million stars converge at her feet.
She walks in beauty, strength and wisdom.
With her by my side, there's no defeat.

Angel of mine, I will love you forever,
For in you, my life's revived and refreshed.
By the waters of Heaven, there's no vision clearer
Than the Light you bring with Joys entrenched.

BEST OF BOTH

The sun shines with magnificence
Like she owns the noon in resplendence,
But today I see a wondrous pair
Of sun and half-moon in luminous affair.

Transfixed by the phenomenon
Of light and dark all seasons long:
Sun at day and moon at night,
There's half-light beaming in my sight!

Best of both from galaxy to earth:
Gardens, hills, valleys, and dregs,
Picking the good from every plane
In life, I say is perfect gain!

Oh sun in my face sweetly dazzling,
And half-moon beside activating
At 3.00pm her nightly chore,
Is nature's mix of tastes galore!

TIME AND LIFE

What is life that wastes its time,
Hampered and shuddered, aged at prime?
What is time that knows not life,
Scampering on highways of peril and strife?

One fair morning, the music began.
Heard across the universe, was a silent clang:
Tick tock, tick tock - resounding in vain
For time with no life is borne in pain.

Time measures what life treasures
And it calculates the wasted tremors,
But neither of these can be regained.
When the clock stops, life's gloried or shamed!

Be wise with time - each minute, each second.
Be all that you dream, to none – a 'second'.
Time is all that your life can own:
Moulded or wasted, the choice your own!

FOCUS

Look on Me, my love,
And I'll look on all concerning you:
Like the sun you see above
Dispersing rays on daylight hue.

Take off your shades of puzzlement
At mountains seeming tall.
With head held high, knees unbent,
Come walk on waterfalls.

For the stars, the trees, the violent winds
And yes, the wooden cross
Are steps that pilgrim life shall find,
Till the heavenly host applauds.

So fix your eyes on Me, my love,
And feel my rays of grace
And power reflecting in wider curve,
Till you can see none but my Face.

ONE SUN

From various angles,
Various towns,
We see the sun
Shining down.

We do not search
Or seek her shine.
She finds us anywhere
At her time.

Through many lives
And generations,
She lights and warms
All God's creation.

We need not crave
To see the light,
When all around
Is already bright.

LUTON POETRY SOCIETY (5th Birthday)

Love makes the world go round.
Understanding keeps us sound.
Talents are shared in words profound
Over chocolates and good coffee.
Never forget the photos glee!

Poetry can make you smile a lot,
Outstanding stories with good plot.
Even better than soup in a pot.
Try to come for one meeting,
Rest assured you'll happy be.
Yes, Luton poets are wide and free.

Started off as a couple of friends
Out to share their thoughts and trends.
Counting, it's been five year ends.
In the library conference room, we meet
Every last Saturday of the month and it
Takes a brand new member like
You to boost our Facebook likes.

(An acrostic poem to mark the 5th birthday of Luton Poetry Society, which I founded in June 2011)

RELATIONSHIP WITH THE SUN

SHADES OF LIGHT – GIFTS OF THE SPIRIT

What an amazing mystery to learn
The seven colours that light impels,
In tune with seven wondrous gifts
Bestowed upon us by the Holy Spirit.

Red is apparent, distinctive, strong
Enough to stop cars from moving along.
Wisdom shows her exceptional ways,
Standing out by the work she displays.

Orange - oh how fresh and supple,
Ripening in fruit, vivifying the morning sun,
Like new understanding of treasured fact -
The word of God that forever lasts.

Yellow depicts brightness at noon,
Butterflies, roses and daffodils in full bloom.
Such brightness that streams from good counsel
Bringing fresh hope when all seems a hassle.

Green is life, vivacity, good health,
Blossoming plants that fill up the earth.
Much like fortitude of the mind and body -
To do God's will, be alive and holy.

Blue is newness - the vast sky can tell,
Bluebells in May, deep sea where fishes dwell.
Knowledge of God shines in newness
Unlocking doors to inner happiness.

Indigo, a darker shade of purple tone:
Relaxed, serene, like when one comes home
To the fruits of goodness and in-depth piety,
Showing rich produce in works of charity.

Violet, hmmm…a name that I can take,
Lightened in lilac of bright floral flakes.
The fear of God brings lasting gleam,
Surmounting rays where Wisdom begins.

Shades of Light and Gifts of the Holy Spirit compared:

Red – Wisdom
Orange – Understanding
Yellow – Good Counsel
Green – Fortitude
Blue – Knowledge
Indigo – Piety
Violet – Fear of God

THE BUTTERFLY SONG

Once I saw the butterfly,
And then yet again.
It sang across the rivers by,
I got to know its name.

I saw its fairer face
Encircled by brown wings,
And through flowers of grace,
It played in joyful rings:

The tune like before
On gardens of dreamland,
The tune I want some more
To dance on classical sand.

Our dancing did caress
My skin with sunlit shower,
Like music by Nigel Hess
'Ladies in Lavender'.

The gardens became confetti
As wind blew in flowers,
Spieled by Benedetti
Performing musical wonders.

The butterfly gazed at me
From the echoes of the sun,
And the wind of destiny
Was written in a song.

*(Nicola Benedetti is a classical violinist who lovingly performs Nigel Hess'
Ladies in Lavender)*

PEACEFUL POWER

It's the peace I find in falling snow,
A hymn at Mass that sets me aglow,
The gentle sound of humming birds
I hear at dawn, whilst in my bed.

It's the rays of sun, the beams of moon,
A walk beside the rivers cool.
Poetry's escape from stress and strain.
In loss, to find a brighter gain.

It's the mirrors I see when mirrored in:
Closed in mind's closet, I see everything.
For when visible mirror is blurred by clouds,
Peaceful power, joyful gleam - they scream aloud!

It's the novel tastes of yummy foods.
Intense workout at the gym, I feel so good!
New movies that draw me to higher thoughts,
And reading the bible for answers sought.

It's the peaceful relaxation with Classic FM,
Especially smooth classics from dusk to AM.
To hear the hidden voice of Wisdom
Speaking to me, as to King Solomon.

It's the power of peace that engulfs me
When I let go and let God take the wheel.
It's knowing that destiny basks in glory,
And silence of earth unveils eternity.

It's these daily inspirations I've penned above
All stemming from the bouquet of love,
And countless niceties I treasure within
That set me to go forth in 2015.

(25th Jan 2015, about 4pm at Luton Central Library)

TRANSPARENCY

When you place a transparent glass
On an opaque surface,
You'd go into the surface
And only feel the glass
When you've touched the surface.

When you place a transparent glass
Behind an opaque surface,
You'd see and feel the surface
Atop a hidden glass.
All I want is surface.

Keep your transparency behind.
Let me see the real you
When I see and feel you.
Mirror not my mind
To see the reflective you.

Keep your tears before you.
Let me think you're smiling
When you're far from smiling,
Till I'm close to see you,
Till I'm why you're smiling.

MY FRIEND, THE SUN

I saw you today patting my wall
Through my kitchen window, when I sang.
In a whole new way, you heard my call
And words from my heart gave heaven a clang.

Timeless sun, you were here from creation,
Ageless, immeasurable, lighting earth's plane,
Giving warmth and life to all generations
And suddenly I realise you know my name.

"Nella Fantasia, io vedo un mundo gusto"
Was the song line that brought your tender gleam:
"In my fantasy, I see a world beautifully so."
And now in my eyes, the sun has come real.

Three times in count, you heard me and shone.
You showed me that light comes only by faith.
My friend, my sun, our thrill has just begun.
I intend to find you where next you await!

(Written on 20th July 2013)

DATE

I said I was coming to meet you
In my very flat shoes,
Walking up the hilly way
On a bright sunny day.

The trees are taller than all else,
Announcing my medium self.
This is going to be a good date,
Best I hurry and not be late.

But hey, you are here already
And you can hear the poem I'm writing,
My timeless sun – up in space!
I can see your glistening face.

I hope that I don't forget
Or edit it much as yet,
For when I get to Stockwood Park,
You'll fill in the words I lack.

(My first day going to write in Stockwood Park on 1st August 2013. It became routine afterwards.)

MEETING YOU

Is it just me or it's breezing
Much more as I'm arriving?
The trees are waving with joy
In tunes that I enjoy.

The sound and priceless sight
When nature comes alight
Beneath the warming sun,
Is that for which I long.

Sitting here now, I wonder,
Could nature be mine so yonder?
The pebbled stones and rocks,
And the soothing wind that talks?

God made them all with love:
The grass, the flowers and dove.
Out here, I can relax
For the trees know me at last.

AFTER PARK

Hello tree!
It's only me.
The park is now closed,
Evening unfolds.

It's still sunny,
Well you can see.
So I'll seat by you:
The shade you drew.

I'd love a little climb
If fruits I'll find,
For life calculates
To activate.

Have to get it right,
Avoid the plight.
Yet you stay strong
All seasons long.

STONES

Pebbles of beauty littering around,
Stones of many shapes, in colours profound:
Ash, grey, brown, cream.
They cluster and glitter in sunlight gleam.

Some are valued and mandatory guests
At birthdays and engagements, from fingers to chest.
But many are chiselled into building foundations,
Cemented, shattered – the wonder of creation!

Yet in my palms, I feel their story:
The screeching sound of nature's symphony.
We are all connected, from stones to high trees,
Nourished by sunlight, rain and the breeze.

Stones, stones, however many you are,
You glaze the earth from near and far.
Trampled or treasured, you remain priceless,
For you are the crux of nature's quintessence.

(Written in Stockwood Park Luton)

BLESS THE LORD

I will bless the Lord at all times,
His praise always on my lips.
My soul cascades with joyful rhymes
To God, my saviour and my keep.

Glorify the Lord with me,
Together let's praise his holy name.
From my distress he set me free
And to my call, his rescue came.

Look towards him and be radiant,
Let not your faces be abashed.
This poor lady on God was reliant,
And all my plea he gently answered.

The angel of the Lord is firmly encamped
Around those who revere him, to rescue them.
Taste his goodness and be steeped
Into his grace - him refuge of men.

Revere the Lord, O you his saints,
For they lack nothing those who revere him.
Strong lions grow weary and glumly faint,
But those who seek God lack no blessing.

(Based on Psalm 34: verses 1 - 10 in the Bible)

HORSE RIDING

Lady riding on a horse
Toddle, toddle in half circles,
With helmet on to keep from falling
If little rocks from low come calling.

She's riding away in felicity
Through parks and paths, town and city:
The wind caressing her happy hair
Underneath the sun where all is clear.

No stopping to look at dregs and dungeon,
Pickled thorns and shifty chameleons.
How soft and safe her horse's back
To raise her feet where lands do crack.

The sun shines on, illuminating her skin
From pores to veins to thoughts within,
To the soul where God's light elevates.
Through lands and journey, His grace rejuvenates.

THE SUN RENEWS

PERCEPTION

You never know where the sun will rise:
High up the sky or deep in my eyes,
Behind the closets of shattered glass
Or seated with me, here at Mass.

You never know when she'd walk with you
In winding roads of clustered blue.
When her light usurps the dim perception,
You find your feet on hills of perfection.

But you'll never see how much light there is
When you shield from sun that dazzles your iris,
When sleep is preferred to chary brightness
And hope deferred by coated blindness.

FINGERPRINTS

In the crime of passion, your fingerprints I find
Hallmarked across the surface of time.
Permanently plastered is the smile you left behind,
A gesture of kindness in beauty sublime.

It may be coincidence but evidence do tell
The sequence of events unfolding in turns.
From hand to hand, there's ringing of bells -
One step to the next as destiny unfurls.

Your fingerprints remain seen or unseen,
Felt much more from the silent source.
You were here, standing tall above the rim
Where reasonable doubt has no recourse.

In warmth and vapour, you are revealed:
I hold you close, take you everywhere!
Your fingerprints can only be cleaned
By forgetfulness, and that I couldn't bear!

LIGHT AND DARKNESS

Light ever subdues the darkness,
It always does, leaving out none
But light and truth. Holiness
Is not subjugated to pits forlorn.

Holiness embraces fair-faced acts
With purer intention and peaceful mind,
And never in time were falsehood marks
Detected on the face of love divine.

An attempt to shield the deceptive oil
In a vast sea of purity, makes revealed
The sordid marks that must recoil
To nothingness, quashed, forever repealed!

Light is light without the darkness
And darkness in light is crushed in fullness!

BEYOND (Acrostic poem)

Beyond
Every
Yes
Or
No,
Discern.

I'M YOUR ANGEL

From you, I sought a sign to see,
Such to prove you're here with me.
My faith was strong but love in lack
As mountains felled upon my back.

I needed to rise on angel's wings,
You voice to hear in celestial ring!
Talk to me today, my love,
If you guide me still from heaven above.

Not once, but twice, my proof arose
From a forgotten, searching, deserted rose.
When nothing else stood along the way,
You took my hand, I heard you say:

"I'm your angel." That soothing sound
By word and deed was so profound.
"I'm your angel" - the best there is
Of a message from whom I really miss.

I look now to the sky that beams inside
With rays unending for all my stride.
Now I know that everything to come
Illuminates in you, you bright as sun!

DISINFECT

Don't allow the effect
Of past woes reflect
On the present good
Happening to you.

(13th September 2014)

NEW DIMENSION

Just close your eyes, reach for the sun,
Remember you're the chosen one.
Let the wind blow, caress your skin
And the rain revitalise your being.

How sweet and crunchy chocolate can be,
Greener inside, full of love – do you see
The timIng of newness and swift realisation
That old stocks must go, for rejuvenation?

Detach from the past to attach with joy
To the new you…real you…running *ahoy*!
On the treadmill of destiny, it's forward ever
Till you grasp the star that shines forever.

The star is in you, reflecting outside
On a new dimension of glamorous tide.
Look again, live again and never stop
Till divinity descends in a glorious cup.

SEQUENCE

Tensed
Stressed
Oppressed
Suppressed
Repressed
Depressed.

Reloaded
Recreated
Motivated
Invigorated
Elevated
Rejuvenated!

(Try reciting it with piano sounds after each line!)

PENTECOST

Light up a candle and it stays lit,
Giving out glow and fervent heat.
Stretch out your hands to receive the dove.
On your head, tongues of fire from above.

Refrain: Veni Creator Spiritu! Come, Holy Spirit, come!

For when the Spirit comes to you,
He'll lead you to the complete truth.
The words of Jesus, he'll steadily remind.
Great things to come, he'll bring to your mind.

He brings forth peace to restless hearts.
His resplendent light in us never departs.
Fill us, Holy Spirit, till we can feel
None else but you, and through you to feel.

Bring peace, bring grace and unwavering power
To all that long for your ceaseless shower.
Heal the sick, make strong the weak.
Give wisdom in seasons bright and bleak.

A candle lit is fuelled from inside.
O Holy Spirit, your gifts in us reside!
Through life's voyage, may we not tarry,
But bear rich fruits to God's great glory!

(Pentecost Sunday 8th June 2014)

FOR MY SHAMROCK

Just in case I don't see you again,
Hard to bid farewell and touch regain,
Timely love can cause such pain
That happy tears start falling like rain.

Just in case we run out of luck
Replanting from water to soil, my shamrock,
If forthcoming seasons halt your clock,
I know you'll forever bring me good luck.

On St. Patrick's Day, from valleys of Erin,
I gladly received you from the hands of Noreen.
For thirty days in water, you've been blossoming.
How a little stem grows is truly amazing!

But Pauline reminds me it's time to replant.
A flower pot and compost her kindness did grant.
"Unless a grain falls into the ground, it can't
Grow to a big tree." was my Gospel chant.

I'm replanting you today with undying love,
My little faith to grow into a big tree above.
Of my own name, I'll call you Marigove,
My shamrock! Just promise me you will thrive.

TIME AND CHANCE

Sometimes we remember.
Sometimes we forget.
Sometimes we understand
That life's as good as it gets.

Sometimes we can see,
Oh sometimes we are blind
And the splash of many colours
Eludes from our mind.

It may be in the wind
Or in the winter rain,
Or in the gentle smile that sparks
A candle in your brain.

Unknowingly, unplanned,
The sun begins to shine.
Time and chance forever hold
The secret to life sublime.

SEASONS OF LIFE

RAIN ON ME

I'm standing in the mud, my feet drenched
In the frothy waters of blocked bath stench,
Encircling and rising like wasted stream,
With no certain passage or intention to flee.

But in the sky, it's raining - the bathroom shower
Is gushing with splendour clean, warm water,
And the rounded sun shines through the rain.
My bathroom bulb illuminating my terrain.

My lips start to move in joyful song,
My legs gliding in soap and smog:
"From all that dwell below the skies,
Let the Creator's praise arise!"

I know not when the filthy waters will clear
But crystal water is running through my hair,
So I'm praising and lifting God's name in glory
Who lifts me from troubles, re-writes my story.

(Thoughts in the Bathroom. The sun is likened to yellow light bulb and rain likened to water gushing from the shower head!)

CARE OR DARE

I try not to care
And pretend you're not there,
But the little truth behind
Is it's you on my mind.

Beside that friendship nest
Is hung the deeper quest,
For I know that in the sun,
Your voice is my song,

And your eyes seek me out
To what love is all about.
I could dare, I could dare…
I won't care, I do care.

In your heart of pure gold,
I find wisdom untold
But I'm fluffed if I should care
And lay my sentiments bare.

I can tell that you know
It's either me or the snow,
So I dare you to call
And find in me your all.

FORESIGHT

If you could see what glory lies ahead,
Would you lurk in dark valleys instead?
Eating the dust of fruitless worry
Or get carried away in a depressive lorry?

Would you climb the mountain seeming high,
Knowing that grace comes when you try?
Or slt back and wait till the weather's right?
Light in darkness is brighter Light!

Twice is made the journey that stops
At fleeting pains and fretful burps,
When destination cries for wholesomeness
That you may arrive in healthiness.

If you could breathe the inner cool ventilation
And exhale the flutters of desolation,
You'll see that mountain eventually become
The vital stairway that leads to the sun.

REMEMBER

I remember the first time I wrote a poem:
I thought about big words, I flipped a pen.
I didn't care if I'd make sense or not,
I had to say my feelings in a secret plot.

My poem was about love, as you can guess.
Such a huge topic for a teenager to address.
I said my heart was 'noble' and that love surely
Was reciprocated – does that sound poorly?

You see, I had my wonderland vision of love
That gave my first poem the wings of a dove.
I still write like this today, a merge of reality
And fantasy - shedding light on life's perplexity.

I remember many things, I remember to remember
And when I forget to forget, I realise I remember,
And when National Poetry Day has come and gone,
I'll wonder how many memories the nation has spun.

(Written for National Poetry Day 2014 on the theme 'Remember')

CINEMA

The cinema is now closed
And the real story has begun.
The drama that you supposed
Was true, ne'er did belong.

Soundtracks and pictures
With many emotions to go
Were but transitory features.
True stories end in snow!

So pick the remnants quietly:
Your popcorn and finished drink.
Walk the walk confidently,
Shut doors and never think.

In time, you'll find that deep within,
A better tale is set to start.
You paid the price to see a film,
Paid with your tender heart.

SHELTERING THE WEATHER

Once
Among the good ones,
A reason
Has arisen
As to whether
The fluctuating weather
Creates a pane
Of looming pain
From your mounting
That mountain
That seemed so red
Before you read
What you now hear
Over here,

You may want to wait
And check the weight
Of the lid
Covering your lead,
To clearly see
If the painful sea
Filing now your plate
Is lighter than the plait
Girding your waist.
For it will be waste
If your happiness check
Is zeroed on a cheque
And you are reaching still
For that which does your joy steal!

(This poem rhymes in homophones - that is two words that are pronounced the same way, but have different letters and different meanings.)

LEAP YEAR

Some things I cannot get enough.
Some things I'd like to come my way.
Some things I have to let go of:
Thoughts arising on the extra day.

Never enough time to finally decide
What to do and what not to do.
Tasks that puddle into the eventide,
Questions and choices for me and you?

Well, how about I give and do as I please,
Take the lessons and reap the produce?
Undo, redo, retrieve, and release
Till next leap year comes – I'll keep my muse.

(Written on 29th February 2016)

WHAT WILL DAISY DO?

What will daisy do
Without her yellow dress
And all her glittering rest?
When the summer's blue
And winter's new,
O what will daisy do?

What will daisy say
When icy winds do blow
And pale is sunset show?
When the light of sun
Is so long gone,
O what will daisy say?

How will daisy cope
When lands become a heath
And thorns draw from beneath?
With her inner shine
And strength divine,
O she is sure to cope!

(Photo of a lovely yellow bush daisy in my neighbour's garden. I admired it all summer 2013, until it was cut down!)

CERTAINTY

The sun still arises
Above this leafy tree.
The flowery top it brightens
While the low stays green,
And where the sun enlightens
No shades could ever dim.

The tree of life is growing
Despite the chokes of lower weeds.
Though sun may seem a-moving
And rain from sky impedes,
The wisdom flower keeps glowing
For the voice of sun she heeds.

SUNNY EYES

You dazzle me. Oh you dazzle me!
You make so bright the things I see.
I gaze on you, you're smiling back,
You leave me a blinding sunny patch.

Sun-struck by you, I mope around
Can't see a thing from sky to ground,
Without the patch of your jealous love
Duly stamped on them thereof!

I close my eyes, you're locked inside,
My heart starts to glow like it's yuletide.
My skin so warm from midday romance
Where memories of rain don't stand a chance!

To see your light everywhere I go
To feel your warmth when it starts to snow,
My friend, my Sun, is a pact we make.
You'll preserve me when seasons quake.

THE SUN AND FAMILY

BUTTERFLY

Freely, freely, I travel by
From gentle lands to mountains high.
Come to me in summer wind
And leave the puzzled world behind.

I'm fragile and sweet
Buttered and swift,
I fly where I choose
My life's an endless cruise.

I stop for a sip from nectar's cup.
Nothing deluded can make me stop.
I find my peak in summertime
On peaceful gardens, I recline.

I'm undisturbed by wandering hands.
My enthusiasm, they can't withstand.
I'd sprinkle colours on their skin
Who try to pluck my patterned wings.

I'm one for many adventures to come
Flying freely under the sun.
I live my life in full supply
Buttered and sweet, I'm butterfly.

INTO THE WOODS

Cinderella was bored, lonely and sad:
Too many chores, they'll drive a person mad!
So she thought she'd go dancing, let her hair down
And she found her prince from way out of town.

Rapunzel was pretty, with long golden hair,
To whomever she chooses they'd form a stair!
A prince said "Rapunzel, you've stolen my heart,
Let down your hair and I'll climb up your path."

Little red riding hood had a basket full of bread
Hopping off joyfully to poor grandma's shed.
Big bad wolf got in the way and ate them both for lunch.
Oh they tore his stomach, red hood was good with punch!

And Jack, oh he threw away his magic beans,
They grew to the sky - climb up if you please?
Touch the moon, reach destiny, hold nothing back,
For muse is found when you think you lack!

You see the new movie "Into The Woods"
Garnished with flowers and trees bad and good,
Has taught me to reach high and take simple steps
For destiny unfurls when winding paths intercept.

(17th January 2015, about 3pm)

A TIMELESS SONNET

You promised me in happy tone
That you will be a poet
When you grow up – oh like sweet cologne,
Your encouragement was my best sonnet!

My dearest Uncle, I didn't realise
That those were your last words to me,
For God has called you to eternal sunrise
Free from pain of mortality.

Yet words are timeless and brighter still
Are the footprints you left on wisdom's lane,
So I'll keep your memory on ceaseless refill
Till seasons past, we meet again.

To you, I present this poetry rosette
Assembled in letters of a timeless sonnet.

(For uncle Ugwum Ezeigbo, R.I.P)

MOON

I'm watching the moon in the sky moving
Or is it just the clouds shifting?
There's moon in my eyes, softly reflected
In beams by which we are connected.

What sees you is what you see:
Eye to eye, drawing from within.
No word or sound could ever suffice
The visual sentiment starting to rise.

You're a planet, somewhere beyond
But from my window, I see a bond
That requires no shuttle or astronaut
To conclude the love that we have caught.

Surrounded by clouds, with light blue spine
Encircling the circumference of your shine,
I fall asleep with moon on my mind
And you in my eyeballs redesigned.

(Thursday 22nd August 2013 – sometime around 11pm, and yes I couldn't sleep until I finished the poem!)

MELODY FIRE

I'd like to box the melody
For each sound is perfection,
Take it away deep in my heart
Cascading tunes of passion.

Like flashing rays of twilight sun
And stars that rain at dusk,
The piano sent lightening waves
For emotions to unmask.

From serenity to fire and back again,
Franz Liszt to Beethoven's sonata,
Melody drove the wind tonight
Skilfully played by Fiachra.

I've fallen in love with music
And it breaks my heart to hear
That when the velvet curtain's drawn,
The music disappears!

LAST DANCE

Sway with me by the patterns of night
On a crystal ocean reflecting our delight.
Everything comes alive at sunset glow:
The gardens of peace, wherever we go.

Hold my hands, unlock my dreams,
Oh feel the rhythm of silent scream.
If the sky could sing, will it outpour
The years gone by and memories restore?

The moon river verily cascades in my eyes
Flooding the reality of vanishing ice
As the ocean melts with the rise of sun,
Dried up are memories regained at dusk.

In eternity's moment, life comes alive:
Past friends and relatives held dear in love.
So dance with me up the stairway of light
Till we catch a glimpse of heaven's delight.

ENSCONCED

MARY: How do you take thine coffee, fair friend?

WILLIAM: That millions of strange shadows on you tend?

MARY: What sayest thou, that thou art still here?

WILLIAM: Against that time do I ensconce me here.

MARY: Sitting beside me in a shelf, I thee find.

WILLIAM: Since I left thee, mine eye is in my mind.

MARY: Oh sometimes, I do feel thy shadows find me.

WILLIAM: The very part was consecrate to thee.

MARY: Tell me, William, how doth love our times renew?

WILLIAM: How can it? O how can love's eye be true?

MARY: In words and thought, I hold thee so near.

WILLIAM: Thou best of dearest, and mine only care!

WILLIAM: The sun itself sees not, till heaven clears

MARY: And shadows away, you are mine, nay fears!

(Written on Monday 25th April 2016, two days after William's birthday on 23rd April. I was having coffee in White House Luton and reading my book of Shakespeare's Sonnets, and when I looked at the Book Shelf beside me, there was the big book "The Complete Works of William Shakespeare". So I bought it from the pub, convinced that William sat beside me for coffee.)

References to William's Words:

Line 2 – Sonnet 53, line 2
Line 4 – Sonnet 49, line 9
Line 6 – Sonnet 113, line 1
Line 8 – Sonnet 74, line 6
Line 10 – Sonnet 148, line 9
Line 12 – Sonnet 48, line 7
Line 13 – Sonnet 148, line 12

DOUBLE THREE

Double the energy exerted on good,
Triple the glory given to God.
Double the powers of Spirit bestowed,
Triple transcendence on this day renewed.

Three persons in God, three days to arise
When at 3pm He died, after thrice Peter denies.
Double the glow of my inward sun -
Jesus my source all seasons long!

Don't double my efforts or triple my pain.
Double my favours and triple my gain.
Double God's grace, mercy and love
To triple my wisdom, healing and thrive.

Double celebration, triple rejuvenation.
Three decades of prayer and silent meditation.
Double my joy, oh triple my peace
To sail tranquil through stormy seas.

Double my blessings flowing from Heaven.
Triple my powers, triple eleven.
Double the double, triple the three.
Double double, three three.

*[In Mathematics: triple eleven = **33**.*
*Double three (3+3=6) + triple three (3x3x3=27) = **33**]*

SUNLESS

I can't quite see you visible as yet,
Though brightness behind the clouds are set
To reveal or retreat in the face of bleak showers.
Will my little hope flood away or tower?

In the midst of unseeing, I feel so much
In memory and longing for your luminous touch.
I know you'll come when the time is right
And knowing surpasses my rain-struck sight.

Everything good, beautiful and true
Certainly outpours from the sky vast and blue,
So I'll fix my gaze on the hopefulness
That like yesterday, today's hung on brightness.

Sunlessly sunny (if ever a phrase like this)
Is how I count the hours for you whom I miss.
No word or contact could ever outclass
The thrill of waiting till sun shines at last.

NIGHT AND DAY

As sure as daylight is to come,
As sure the sunset dawns.
For after light, is darkness told
And light in darkness glows.

One day, one night, a steady count
Each in proportioned amount.
Beneath the sun and moon and stars,
There's pleasure and pain and scars.

From centuries past to those ahead,
The same song has been heard
That never in time did life supply
Just day or just the night.

So when it's day, make merry and hay
And at night, do sleep and pray.
Oh pray and trust and worry for none
For the day is sure to come!

THE SUN TRANSCENDS

ANGEL SUN

True Light begins with light and truth
Exposing the works of pulchritude,
Debunking the shadows that kept confined
Some budding flowers and flourishing mind.

Wisdom, clarity, all gleam from heaven
If we trust to see what God has given.
Angels encamp around the fading tree
To nurture its fruits and set them free!

For when the sun shines, shadows unfold
That hide when the night's serene and cold.
But light and truth reveal such darkness
That prior disguised as 'light' in darkness.

Who's to say the garden's past cultivating
When Eden's wonder is merely rejuvenating?
What previous weeds deceived for long,
Before the rise of the Angel Sun?

She broke the fetters for apostles and Peter:
For me, terrains that sway and quiver.
I know she'll show me the path to go
When crossroads diverge to sleet and snow.

My Angel Sun illuminates inside
To light and guard, to rule and guide.
So when some light is really not light,
She'll dazzle and marvel me with true Light!

TO THE COUNTESS

I dreamed I would meet a Countess someday:
I was dining with the Granthams at Downton Abbey.
The show ends on Christmas day at dinner time,
So my dream would've sunk below sublime.

Last month, I was telephoned by a real Countess
Lady Erroll our High Sherriff – oh dear I need a dress
And a hat to attend her Justice Service in Bedford,
Where I'm to read a poem – I may also need a Ford!

Travel sorted! What a beautiful service it was,
Praying and encouraging the servers of Justice's cause.
Good justice system means "they will all go home in peace",
As read by Lord Erroll from 'Exodus' about Moses.

My poem was at dinner – yes, sat at table with the Countess.
Do dreams really come true? You might take a guess!
You see, Lady Erroll told me that God was leading her
To find and invite me, she thought my poem was clever!

Her family was kind, oh we chatted over champagne:
Lord Harry, Hon. Richard and gorgeous Lady Laline Hay.
Lord Erroll was exceptional and made us all smile.
I wish the Errolls a very happy Christmas time!

TWO KINGS

Going out to search for donkeys,
Coming back with royal keys!
Saul, Saul, how neatly planned
Your destiny was in God's own hand.

Weary, you sought to wander back
But your valet suggested another track.
Through woods and bushes, your feet kept moving
Till Samuel had your head anointing.

David the man after God's own heart,
Small and simple, you tended the farm
Till Samuel overlooked your siblings tall
And anointed you king in front of all.

Oh steady my feet, oh focus my eyes
On God the giver of sweet surprise.
Walk in His word, with shield of faith.
His promise to you will not be late.

(Saul and David were kings of Israel.)

QUEEN

Today, I am a queen for once
Coming from Her Majesty's house.
Mary is my mother Queen,
To Elizabeth Windsor's house I've been.
My daughter Elizabeth is ever joyous.

For one day, I could pass the test
Of royalty by simply being my best.
The Queen's Hotel in Finsbury park
Where the moon first arose at dark,
Has somewhat solved a million quest.

My previous home away from home
Visiting England those years ago,
Draws me to whom I used to be.
Oh inner self, can you not see
That wisdom increases as you grow?

I am a queen today and forever.
As I believe, my faith won't waver.
I am a queen with grace and glory,
Not Mary of Scotts or Bloody Mary,
Queen of my very heart!

(Written on 2nd July 2014 in the train back to Luton after visiting Buckingham Palace and Queen's hotel, Finsbury Park)

WITHOUT SUN

Where are you, O sunken sun?
Sunken deep behind the clouds
At night when all the gleam is gone,
And hope but screams aloud.

The wind is cold on gloomy earth
And stars are far from sight,
And all that seemed like lasting wealth
Have vanished in the night.

If I had seen, O brighter sun
That the only source was you,
My faith will stay, my doubts forgone
When morning dawns anew.

O come again, my friend, my sun
And hug me tenderly
With dreams of daylight soon to come,
For how else can I sleep?

LOSING BIG

I don't feel like I have lost,
I have gained at varying cost.
For treasured less
Is swift success
Without a stream of tears outburst.

Lessons learnt are diamonds spread,
Infinitely hung around my head:
My steps to guide
My tongue to chide
When villainous traps are set ahead.

Better the seed that fell into ground
And grew to a tree where birds abound,
Than summer weed
That sprout in speed
From nowhere, now shovelled - all around.

USURPED BY LIGHT

I think I have been usurped by Light
Totally consumed in spite of sight.
All is blurry – the darkness and fog
Before the sunlit face of the Son of God.

The brightest white became His raiment
In a glorious flash on my hill of discernment,
And all came clear when from the sky
The voice of God resonated on high:

"This is my son, the beloved." He declared,
"Listen to him." – my soul has heard,
And from now on I wish to remain
Within your tent on your holy mountain.

Indeed, I have been usurped by Light
And safest now from struggles and plight.
The eternal foretaste of inward sun
Will constantly shine - till to You, I come.

TRANSCENDENCE

There's a little world inside you
Unseen to the eyes, felt deep inside
Like a gust of wind breezing through.
From nowhere, the elements start to collide:

Protons, electrons, memories and forecasts
Swaying around in breeze propellant.
You're here and there, gravity surpassed
Like Lucy's brain capacity at 100 percent!

The wind is gusting but earth is still,
The visible world now becoming iridescent.
Your brain is soaring above trees and hills
To the sky high point where you're transcendent.

There, King Solomon's wisdom shines in corona.
Through the sun, the mind is fully energised.
Now you see and feel everything, the aura
So different from what the human eye disguised.

Behold the hidden secrets of the wind:
By air, we remit immeasurable quotient.
Yet when you start to doubt or rescind,
The inner world stops - and you forget!

(Inspired by King Solomon, and the new movie 'Lucy' about the possibility of human brain capacity reaching 100%)

SUN, MOON AND STARS

She stands in-between time and space
Upon the moon, clothed with the sun.
The stars that scintillate her loving face
And woven into celestial crown.

She feels the warmth of sun inside,
The light of moon when all is dark.
She reads the stars like celestial bride
Deciphering where God has made His mark.

She bore God's Son and Saviour of the world:
The Light for all who follow His way,
The truth and justice when all is flawed,
Whose precepts gladden the heart with rays.

She loves Her Son, who is her King.
He reigns and rains on her with Light
And warmth and strength deep within
To shed His radiance on fading fright.

She is the Queen, and she's the princess
Whose royal bestowment She did install.
She is Mary, Mother of Christ to bless.
I am Mary, daughter of Christ, my all.

(In Revelation Chapter 12:1 Mary Mother of God stands on the moon, clothed with the sun and a crown of twelve stars. The other Mary in verses 2 and 4 refer to me.)

DUSK

When darkness roams across the waters
And birds travel in twilight flutters,
The tree gently tilts to a calm curvature
At rest with the evening shades of nature,
And the fading sun in her last breath of light
Whispers to earth - a kiss goodnight.

DREAM A LITTLE....

Believe in your dreams.
Be living your dreams.

I am a part from Sun.
I am apart from Sun.